The Forward Book
of Poetry 1996

FORWARD PUBLISHING
LONDON

First published in Great Britain by
Forward Publishing · 5 Great Pulteney Street · London W1R 4LD
in association with
Faber and Faber · 3 Queen Square · London WC1N 3AU

ISBN 0 571 17634 8 (paperback)

Compilation copyright © Forward Publishing 1995
For copyright on individual poems see acknowledgements page 7
Foreword copyright © Carol Ann Duffy 1995
Front cover illustration by Maggie Jennings

Typesetting by Graphic Ideas
Karen House · 1-11 Baches Street · London N1 6DL

Printed by Redwood Books Ltd.
Kennet House · Kennet Way · Trowbridge · Wilts. BA14 8RN

A CIP catalogue reference for this book
is available at the British Library.

To N.M.

Preface

THE FOURTH FORWARD BOOK OF POETRY is filled with some of the best
entries to this year's Forward Poetry prizes. Our annual anthologies
are rapidly becoming bestsellers in the growing world of poetry. Last
year, the Forward Book of Poetry made it into the *Sunday Times*
bestseller list, and at the time of writing, had sold over 6,000 copies.
Proceeds from the sale of this anthology go to the Forward Poetry
Trust, a new charitable trust which administers both the prizes and
National Poetry Day.

This year's anthology is published on 12th October 1995, when
Britain will celebrate its second National Poetry Day. All over the
country, in schools, workplaces, railway stations, and over the nation's
airwaves, poetry will be performed and heard; and it is fitting that it
should be so widely celebrated. For, despite many people's perception
that it is a crusty art form confined to the corners of bookshops, poetry
is alive, well and kicking. You'll find it in our popular music, our
advertising, our greetings cards and all through our daily life. We hope
that the work of the Forward Poetry Trust will help to dispel any
remaining prejudice people have about the role of poetry in their life,
and will continue to encourage the remarkable growth of enthusiasm for
poetry that we are experiencing in the last few years of the millennium.

I would like to thank the other organisations and individuals that
helped to make the Forward Poetry Prizes and National Poetry Day
possible; Gordon Kerr at Waterstone's, Jeffery Tolman at Tolman
Cunard and Alastair Niven at the Arts Council of England, whose
funding makes a tremendous contribution to both events. I would also
like to thank the BBC, the Poetry Society and Colman Getty for their
hard work and committed support for National Poetry Day and all those
at Forward Publishing whose enthusiasm has helped to produce this
anthology. Last but not least, may I record my heartfelt gratitude to our
five judges, Rosie Boycott, Alan Jenkins, Lord Gowrie, Carol Ann Duffy
and Peter Forbes, who conscientiously read mountains of poetry and
selected this wonderful anthology from them.

William Sieghart

Foreword

THESE ARE TIMES when, to re-write the words of Adrian Mitchell, most poetry no longer ignores most people. The Forward Prizes have, in four brief years, turned a spotlight on contemporary poetry which is both searching and glamorous. Just as important to the organisers of the awards is the annual Forward anthology, which seeks to present a generous selection of poems drawn from the many poetry collections and individual poems submitted by the large publishing houses, small presses, editors, newsapers, quarterlies and little magazines. The poems contained in this year's anthology represent a broad, enthusiastic look at the poetry year, as seen through the eyes of the 1995 judges – Rosie Boycott, Peter Forbes, myself, Lord Gowrie and last year's recipient of the prize for Best Collection, Alan Jenkins.

As with previous Forward anthologies, the shortlisted books and poems from three categories of prize provide a strong selection of opening poems. The five men and five women nominated for Best Collection and Best First Collection range from R.S. Thomas and Iain Crichton Smith – senior poets both, whose work possesses an acknowledged international stature – to Maggie Hannan and Deryn Rees-Jones, young women in their early twenties. The shortlists of five books in these two categories were sweated out on a fiercely hot July day in Soho. There followed the choosing of the poems for the Best Individual Poem prize – a process which yielded not only new work by Seamus Heaney and Les Murray, but saw two vital little magazines, The Rialto and The North, which do so much work in encouraging new poets, impressively represented by Sally Baker and Jenny Joseph.

Nearly fifty other poets are also featured in this year's anthology. All of them provided the judges with something to admire, or quote, or be moved by – whether it be in the form of impressive new collections from Carole Satyamurti, Glyn Maxwell and Michael Longley, or first books from Ann Gray and Katherine Pierpoint. The surrealist David Gascoyne, whose commitment to poetry has lasted a lifetime, is here; as is Neil Astley, the founder of Bloodaxe Books, a press which has been exemplary in recent years in bringing new poetry to its increasingly growing audience.

The 1996 Forward Book of Poetry, published on National Poetry Day, is for that audience. An audience which seeks poetry privately – alone with a book, on the radio, in a Sunday newspaper; or publicly – at a pub reading, strap-hanging on the tube, at festivals. I know I speak also for my fellow judges when I say that it has been a pleasure to choose this selection from a typically varied, moving, funny, clamorous year in poetry. Enjoy.

Carol Ann Duffy

Acknowledgements

Simon Armitage · THE TWO OF US · AFTERWORD · *The Dead Sea Poems* ·
Faber and Faber

Neil Astley · THE HOUND OF THE BASKERVILLES · *Biting My Tongue* ·
Bloodaxe Books

Annemarie Austin · GOAT SONG · *The Flaying of Marsyas* · Bloodaxe Books

Sally Baker · FAKE LEOPARDSKIN COAT · *The North 15*

Connie Bensley · PERSONAL COLUMN · *Choosing To Be a Swan* · Bloodaxe Books

Sujata Bhatt · FRIGHTENED BEES · THE STINKING ROSE · *The Stinking Rose* ·
Carcanet Press

Charles Boyle · VELCRO · *London Review of Books*

Alison Brackenbury · HAY FEVER · *1829* · Carcanet Press

John Burnside · HOME MOVIE · *Times Literary Supplement*

Barry Butson · JUST ANOTHER HIERONYMUS BOSCH EVENING IN WOODSTOCK ·
Planet

Julia Casterton · VIPERS IN LOVE · *London Magazine*

Linda Chase · YOUNG MEN DANCING · *Young Men Dancing* ·
Smith/Doorstop Books

Iain Crichton Smith · DOGMAS · COME, FOOL · *Ends and Beginnings* ·
Carcanet Press

Kwame Dawes · COMMUNION · *Prophets* · Peepal Tree

Rita Dove · BLUE DAYS · *Mother Love* · W. W. Norton & Co

Jane Duran · THE WONDERFUL BELLY DANCE OF RABAH SAÏD · GREAT
GRANDFATHERS · *Breathe Now, Breathe* · Enitharmon Press

Jennie Fontana · EYE OF THE HURRICANE · *Lost Stations* · Stride Publications

Cliff Forshaw · A GOD PERHAPS · *Strange Tongues* · Weasel Productions

David Gascoyne · A SARUM SESTINA · *Selected Poems* · Enitharmon Press

Ann Gray · TIME · *Painting Skin* · Fatchance Press

Sophie Hannah · THE MYSTERY OF THE MISSING · *The Hero and the Girl Next
Door* · Carcanet Press

Maggie Hannan · GOODBYE JONES · APOCRYPHAL · *Liar, Jones* · Bloodaxe Books

Robert Rehder · ON THE NATURE OF PHYSICAL LAW · *The Compromises will be Different* · Carcanet Press

Maurice Riordan · LAST CALL · *A Word From the Loki* · Faber and Faber

Ann Sansom · MINE HOST · *Romance* · Bloodaxe Books

May Sarton · MELANCHOLY · *Coming into Eighty and Earlier Poems* · The Women's Press

Carole Satyamurti · STRIKING DISTANCE · *Striking Distance* · Oxford University Press

Robert Saxton · THE FARMYARD CROCODILE · *The Promise Clinic* · Enitharmon Press

Adam Schwartzman · LIBERAL · *The Good Life. The Dirty Life. And other stories* · Carcanet Press

Penelope Shuttle · OUTGROWN · *The Observer*

Charles Simic · HISTORY LESSON · *Frightening Toys* · Faber and Faber

Matt Simpson · PRUFROCK SCOUSED · *Catching Up With History* · Bloodaxe Books

Harry Smart · OUR PRETTY GARDEN · *Fool's Pardon* · Faber and Faber

Sam Smith · IMPORTANT INFORMATION FOR CANOEISTS · *Odyssey 16*

R. S. Thomas · GERIATRIC · REFLECTIONS · *No Truce with the Furies* · Bloodaxe Books

Charles Tomlinson · WEATHER REPORT · *Jubilation* · Oxford University Press

Greg Woods · A BLIND MAN LOOKS AT A BOY · *Poetry News Review 100*

Gerard Woodward · THE STARTER · *After The Deafening* · Chatto & Windus

9

Contents

The Best Collection Poems

Simon Armitage

Fact: the world will be fixed
in the eyes of friends
who head out west and fetch up
back at home again.

It's that Einstein thing
where one of two twins
takes off for a spin
and returns in the spring

to the place of his birth
with a gift for his brother.
And they see for themselves,
each eyeing the other

through a telescope now
which had once been a mirror.

The Two of Us
(after Laycock)

You sat sitting in your country seat
with maidens, servants waiting hand and foot.
You eating swan, crustaceans, starters, seconds, sweet.
You dressed for dinner, worsted, made to measure. Cut:
me darning socks, me lodging at the gate,
me stewing turnips, beet, one spud,
a badger bone. Turf squealing in the grate –
no coal, no wood.

No good. You in your splendour: leather,
rhinestone, ermine, snakeskin, satin, silk,
a felt hat finished with a dodo feather.
Someone's seen you swimming lengths in gold-top milk.
Me parched, me in a donkey jacket,
brewing tea from sawdust mashed in cuckoo spit,
me waiting for the peaks to melt, the rain to racket
on the metal roof, they sky to split,

and you on-stream, piped-up, plugged-in, you worth a mint
and tighter than a turtle's snatch.
Me making light of making do with peat and flint
for heat, a glow-worm for a reading lamp. No match.
The valleys where the game is, where the maize is –
yours. I've got this plot just six foot long
by three foot wide, for greens for now, for daisies
when I'm dead and gone.

You've got the lot, the full set:
chopper, Roller, horse-drawn carriage, microlight, skidoo,
a rosewood yacht, a private jet.
I'm all for saying that you're fucking loaded, you.
And me, I clomp about on foot from field to street;
these clogs I'm shod with, held together now with segs
and fashioned for my father's father's father's feet –

they're on their last legs.

Some in the village reckon we're alike, akin:
same neck, same chin. Up close that's what they've found,
some sameness in the skin,
or else they've tapped me on the back and you've turned round.
Same seed, they say, same shoot,
like I'm some cutting taken from the tree,
like I'm some twig related to the root.
But I can't see it, me.

So when it comes to nailing down the lid
if I were you I wouldn't go with nothing.
Pick some goods and chattels, bits and bobs like Tutankhamen
   did,
and have them planted in the coffin.
Opera glasses, fob-watch, fountain pen, a case of fishing flies,
a silver name-tag necklace full-stopped with a precious stone,
a pair of one pound coins to plug the eyes,
a credit card, a mobile phone,

some sentimental piece of earthenware,
a collar stud, a cufflink and a tiepin,
thirteen things to stand the wear and tear
of seasons underground, and I'll take what I'm standing up in.
That way, on the day they dig us out
they'll know that you were something really fucking fine
and I was nowt.
Keep that in mind,

because the worm won't know your make of bone from mine.

Sujata Bhatt

FRIGHTENED BEES
Notes from a Welsh Herbal

Take a clove of garlic
prick in three or four places in the middle
dip in honey and insert in the ear
covering it with some black wool.

And if I had no black wool
would white wool do –
or must it be at least red
or dark blue?

Let the patient sleep
on the other side every night
leaving the clove in the ear
for seven or eight nights unchanged.
It will prevent the running of the nose
and restore the hearing.

Black wool I found at last
but it makes me dream
of frightened bees with a dead queen –
      homeless
swarms rushing in a panic –

night after night – the dead queens
are piling up fast – but someone wants
to crush them with rose petals
and honey – someone wants to eat
the dead queens and taste
a sweetness,
      a knowledge no one dares to try.

THE STINKING ROSE

Everything I want to say is
in that name
for these cloves of garlic – they shine
like pearls still warm from a woman's neck.

My fingernail nudges and nicks
the smell open, a round smell
      that spirals up. Are you hungry?
Does it burn through your ears?

Did you know some cloves were planted
near the coral-coloured roses
to provoke the petals
into giving stronger perfume...

Everything is in that name
      for garlic:
Roses and smells
      and the art of naming...

What's in a name? that which we call a rose,
By any other name would smell as sweet...

But that which we call garlic
smells sweeter, more
vulnerable, even delicate
if we call it *The Stinking Rose.*

The roses on the table, the garlic in the salad
and the salt teases our ritual
tasting to last longer.
You who dined with us tonight,
this garlic will sing to your heart
to your slippery muscles – will keep
your nipples and your legs from sleeping.

Fragrant blood full of garlic –
yes, they noted it reeked under the microscope.

His fingers tired after peeling and crushing
the stinking rose, the sticky cloves –
Still, in the middle of the night his fingernail
nudges and nicks her very own smell
        her prism open –

Iain Crichton Smith

Come, Fool

Come, fool, and tell me of your successes
just here where the wind combs the grasses
by this cemetery with its wooden crosses.

Come, gold-buttoned fool, with your new car
shining like a crab: walk over
this ancestral ground with its white flowers,

and talk in your loud voice of your gains,
your Midas jacket. Do you not feel the presence
of the empty-mouthed dead, and the dance

of the extinct girls.
              Come, glassy fool,
stand by this stone and see your own name

excised as in your schooldays, an address
from your poor cottage to the universe

and then to your Mercedes and your hearse.

Dogmas

Perfidious dogmas,
unremitting theses,
let the wild seas
blow through you

with their salt taste
and tang of seaweed
and all the dead
whose bones have been picked clean

by the fresh currents,
and let the rocks of dogma
be steadily worn down
till only the water

brilliantly sparkling
with its modern ships
flows always eastward
towards a temporary sun.

Sean O'Brien

Railway Songs

Trains go past. Their effigies do likewise,
Upstairs on the layout, all afternoon.
The world is private. This is the meaning of weather—
The icicle losing its grip at the roof's edge,
The white afternoons at the far end of summer—
Weather, and trains, with the world indoors,
Advancing its strangeness over the lino.

Squint through your specs, through the fog,
Through the downpour, the clear-eyed dawn of October,
At actual engines departing the city,
Intent on the serious north. No flock-grass
Or papier-mâché, tunnel, viaduct
Or working prewar German water-mill
Can take you there, yet you believe
In the place where the points are iced over
And wolves have got into the signal-box,
Leaving their pawprints across the slick parquet
And windows steamed over with signalmen's terror.

Delight, as you crouch by the paraffin heater
And idly unravel your cable-stitch pullover.
Oh to be Scotland By Rail, a grey rock
In the shape of a tender, displayed
By a smoke-coloured sea; to have become
The merest fire-blanket in the corridor
When everything falls silent, when the smoke
Has borne itself away above the snowy cutting
With a tunnel at both ends, between
The lapse of conversation and the panic.

*

Rain is vanishing the hills.
All down the line the stations go missing—
Bridges, Markets, Highest Points and Heritage
Undone by rain, the coal-fired weather
Of almost-irreparable newsreel. Whole counties
Turn to smoking stacks of viaducts
From under which, by documentary miracle,
Engines by the dozen steam
In parallel straight at us.

                    *

Here inside this grey-green afternoon
Is where I've always lived. It stretches
From the War until they burn me like a sleeper.

I've stayed on at home. Our railings were stolen
For weapons, they told us, which left low walls
To run like blacked-out carriages

Around the parks and cemeteries.
I'm waiting today in the shelter
While a half-mad gardener explains

How corpses drive his floral clock,
Whose movement is based upon Kilmarnock station.
At the church after service are middle-aged ladies

Who dance through the trees to a small guitar.
But the children are looking at something quite different,
The tracks, perhaps, beyond the hedge,

And the phone in the vestry keeps ringing the once
For the vicar is also this small station's master
And Bradshaw is still in his heaven.

                    *

When the County Grounds are hailed-on and empty
And the miserable old parties who snapped
In Leeds and Sheffield, Middlesbrough and Hull,
'We'll have that wireless off' are dead and stuffed,
The special lines remain between the cricket and their graves.

Likewise 'The masters who taught us are dead',
But we have hung on with our oddments of habit,
Pausing perhaps when the sun strikes the red and green glass
In the porch, or inclined to believe
That the groundsman was made an exception to death

And sits there grinning silently
At *Workers' Playtime* on the wireless in his hut,
With a goods train sliding past just out of earshot.

The Mallard comes steaming out of its frame
And the four-minute mile waits like Everest –
Cinder tracks everywhere, sodden and virtuous,

Coal-coloured sandshoes and wet, gritty legs,
While shunters go by, bringing rain to Hull Fair,
To the trains made of china, the trains full of goldfish,

The half-naked girl-in-a-tank-with-a-train,
The dripping back flap of the Ghost Train,
The driver's mate waving at no one.

The Politics of

When I walk by your house, I spit.
That's not true. I *intend* to.
When you're at breakfast with the *Daily Mail*
Remember me. I'm here about this time,
Disabled by restraint and staring.
But I do not send the bag of excrement,
Decapitate your dog at night,
Or press you to a glass of Paraquat,
Or hang you by your bollocks from a tree,
Still less conceal the small home-made device
Which blows your head off, do I, prat?
I think you'll have to grant me that,
Because I haven't. But I might.
If I were you, I'd be afraid of me.

R.S. Thomas

GERIATRIC

What god is proud
    of this garden
of dead flowers, this underwater
    grotto of humanity,
where limbs wave in invisible
    currents, faces drooping
on dry stalks, voices clawing
    in a last desperate effort
to retain hold? Despite withered
    petals, I recognise
the species: Charcot, Ménière,
    Alzheimer. There are no gardeners
here, caretakers only
    of reason overgrown
by confusion. This body once,
    when it was in bud,
opened to love's kisses. These eyes,
    cloudy with rheum,
were clear pebbles that love's rivulet
    hurried over. Is this
the best Rabbi Ben Ezra
    promised? I come away
comforting myself, as I can,
    that there is another
garden, all dew and fragrance,
    and that these are the brambles
about it we are caught in,
    a sacrifice prepared
by a torn god to a love fiercer
    than we can understand.

REFLECTIONS

The furies are at home
in the mirror; it is their address.
Even the clearest water,
if deep enough can drown.

Never think to surprise them.
Your face approaching ever
so friendly is the white flag
they ignore. There is no truce

with the furies. A mirror's temperature
is always at zero. It is ice
in the veins. Its camera
is an X-ray. It is a chalice

held out to you in
silent communion, where gaspingly
you partake of a shifting
identity never your own.

The Best First Collection Poems

Jane Duran

GREAT GRANDFATHERS
for Henry Crompton

Sometimes you glimpse one –
a great grandfather –
among the trees
with his white hair blown forward
seated and secret,
glad to see you there
only just higher than his knees,
the checkered blanket,
sugar-line of the rivermouth
on his mouth.

You can hardly remember, later.
You were only four when he died
and neither of you in full faculties
when you met, so your greeting
was really a goodbye:
a blanket, leaves, a scrap of beard,
a river happening to a beach,
your heaven against his.

Still, when you think of him
he is tall, he is broad
as if he were set about with himself,
as if all the forests of Lancashire
had been used to build him.
He lones in his age.

His age is becoming fabulous.
Your mother says if he were alive now
he would be 102.
And there is that bundle of letters
he left behind

which you are only allowed to touch
with the delicacy of a ladybird alighting –
so brittle, so see-through.

Great, he is greater than your father,
grandfather, less great than his.
You think of going backward
like the sandpiper chasing the lost wave
wrestling with the tide
adept and forlorn
or how the balloon breath rushes back into
your mouth when you are trying
very hard to blow it up
to take to the park,
how it could blow you all the way back
right against his heart.

The Wonderful Belly Dance of Rabah Saïd

When Rabah dances
in his tiny apartment
on the outskirts of Malmö
his friends round the coffee-table
witness
his belly imperious.

When he shimmies
between the television set
and the picture window

landmarks surface out of the fog.
At the black docks
the lights of the ferry to Copenhagen
turn on all at once.

He unbuttons his shirt.
He locks his hands behind his head
whirls and shudders on the spot

and the last stars leap
between branches of fir trees.
Over the fleeting farmlands
barn doors open
to let out their dark.

In sedate parade meanders
the gleam of cattle haunches
and breath has an edge of snow
an edge of sirocco

like two cusps of the moon
when Rabah lifts up his arms
and laughs down at his dancing belly
over the astonished

rooftops of Malmö

and a young bridegroom, lying awake
remembers a riddle
from his childhood
when Rabah spins down the hallway

gliding, eddying
across the marine snow of Sweden:
a sandstorm at dawn,
his red shirt – banners.

Maggie Hannan

APOCRYPHAL

Like butter on water, a tic on the skin
of the lake where it bobs. A limb on a hook,
hauled in by men. A leg with a shoe, with a name.

It is beached and observed: like a fish,
a luminous grey. Unshoe it, unsock it, return
it to town in a truck. Human remains.

Get it a docket. Call in the weeping, who will
bicker like birds at the side of the coffin:
which end to put it. The place of the ruff.

Bury it. Bury it. Dig a hole like a dog does,
then pray like a man, for a man. Leave flowers,
forget it for years, till the day when you're

told of a man who returns to the site
of the grave and a locket of water. Laughter.
A man on a crutch, with a shoe, with that name.

*

I am watching you work. Your eyes wide like
asterisks on the page of your face. You are
reading a book, you say, which poses a question

you cannot unhook. Look, I am quoting: *Someone
is crossing the bridge. But is it me?* You are
scowling, and curling your lip like a line

which is cast to the drowning. No wonder,
at night, you are lifting the covers to see
for yourself what you're like: a sack-full,

a mind-full, a heat and a sweat, the tattoo
of a heart which is yours. You are reading:
If you lost your mind. would you know it?

Goodbye Jones

The noise of the fist will be
the noise of the door, next.

Next to that, the news
on a postcard. A hundred words.

In England, you have found
the perfect flyover... *Near*

Bristol... you write, having
parked the Reliant Robin

by the transport caff and gorge,
spending your last on chips.

You decide: *Today, I'm
ditching gravity. Wish me*

luck... losing your skirts
for the first ascent

to carve your name in stone.
A fortnight later, postmarked

Portugal, a polaroid arrives.
You bless the man, weather,

and sweat you've found,
build houses in the sand.

I am finding myself...
Liar, Jones. Call me...

Thankyou, thankyou, thankyou.

Gwyneth Lewis

FROM WELSH ESPIONAGE (PART V)

Welsh was the mother tongue, English was his.
He taught her the body by fetishist quiz,
father and daughter on the bottom stair:
'Dy benelin yw *elbow*, dy wallt di yw *hair*,

chin yw dy ên di, *head* yw dy ben.'
She promptly forgot, made him do it again.
Then he folded her *dwrn* and, calling it fist,
held it to show her knuckles and wrist.

'Let's keep it from Mam, as a special surprise.
Lips are *gwefusau, llygaid* are eyes.'
Each part he touched in their secret game
thrilled as she whispered its English name.

The mother was livid when she was told.
'We agreed, no English till four years old!'
She listened upstairs, her head in a whirl.
Was it such a bad thing to be Daddy's girl?

The Spy Comes Home
From Welsh Espionage (Part VII)

Leave, if you like, but those you've left won't wait
to bear you witness once you've broken free.
Now pay the price for coming home too late.

Warmth I expected, or a loving hate,
the deserter resented for his liberty.
Leave, if you like, but those you've left won't wait.

Peer through the window at the leaded grate,
tap on the pane with the rain-soaked tree.
Now pay the price of coming home too late.

Steal away and time will confiscate
the place you hoarded in your memory.
Leave, if you like, but those you've left won't wait.

Who's to redeem the jaded reprobate,
if not the incurious in the family?
Now pay the price of coming home too late.

A row of graves by the chapel gate,
mouths as cold as their charity.
Leave, if you like, but those you've left won't wait.
Now pay the price of coming home too late.

Justin Quinn

CLEARING
at Zbýšov

After walking miles of forest-path,
        Each hour the same,
    Just able to make out the vague width
      Allowed our feet by fern
Pendent above the dark clay floor, we came
        Into the open.

As though we were the first to walk the earth
        And see this place,
    The twilight's flare on grass and wort,
      First to see the slant
Of sunrays downward, every glance and pause
        Echoed with portent:

Like bulbs, two cities blinked out of existence,
        One twig snapped.
    The rest, caught in one look askance,
      Swung wildly out of tilt –
Road and roof and parliament all upped
        With one huge jolt

To orbit in their proper atmosphere.
        A skyborne chaos
Of concrete, glass, and tangled wire,
      Autoroutes which lurched
In panic like half-murdered snakes: no *deus*
        Ex machina arched

Above our heads. As though cut adrift
        From house and law
    Into this clearing's silence, left
      Once more to our devices,

Released back into clarity, we saw
          Nothing, heard less.

               *

That night, when rain was falling hard against
          The angled pines
    And swept in waves across the forest,
          Through a distant copse,
Strewing in its wake drunk corrugations
          Among the tree-tops,

Broken only by the clearing's naught,
          Its darker disc
    Which made an almost perfect umlaut
          With the nearby pond,
Its surface crackling with an arabesque
          Of rain and wind,

The two of us were safely under roof.
          Whatever stormed
    Above us tried to heave and shove
          The sky's big furniture –
Pylon skidding into pyramid
          On thundering castor –

Into some new arrangement of horizons,
          And us caught there
    In that exchange of sun-ups, mountains,
          Fields turned into clouds and seas,
Our room become an old box camera's chamber
          For strobe-lit trees,

Early newsreels whirring on the walls.
          The bloody changes:
    Militia, desperate for reprisals,
          Flickered up and fired,

Then, turning into bankers, grocers, newsagents,
        They disappeared;

The couple who first owned the house arrested
        On home-movie,
   An eight mil. afternoon which lasted
      Fifty years, embraces
Awkward, quick, their blind bequest the duvet
        Covering us.

Against an outside wall a shutter slams
        Repeatedly.
   And that the basement, bricks, and beams
      Hold true is all we care
To know of this. I check each lock and key
        For love, for fear.

The 'O'o'a'a' Bird

Once there was a time
    I sang in trees,
And forest reached right to the rim
    Of everything that was.

The pristine world spun free
    Of fences then
Without the empty clarity
    Of plaza, field or plan.

My song had origins
    Of bole and sky,
As much as come-ons to the hens,
    Whom I loved, and they me.

(But listen to your music:
    Blasting sennets
From drills at road-works, or asthmatic
    Engines under bonnets,

An electronic chirrup
    When your travel-pass
Is good for one more day, the blip
    You need to know you'll last.)

You couldn't stand our freedom.
    You laid your laws
That silenced us, in this your time
    Of consonants, fences, chainsaws.

Deryn Rees-Jones

LOVESONG TO CAPTAIN JAMES T. KIRK

Captain. I never thought we'd come to this,
but things being what they are, being adults,
stardate '94 it's best to make the best of it
and laugh. What's done is done. Perhaps
I'll start to call you Jim or Jamie, James...

No one was more shocked than me when I arrived
(*the lady doth protest*) to find
my bruised and rainy planet disappeared
and me, materialised and reconstructed
on board the Starship Enterprise, all 60s
with my lacquered bee-hive and my thigh-high
skirt in blue, my Doctor Marten's and my jeans
replaced by skin-tight boots
and scratchy blue-black nylons rippling-
up my less-than-perfect calves. Sulu
looked worried. Spock cocked up one eyebrow
enigmatically, branding my existence
perfectly illogical. How nice, I thought. His ears.
Uhura smiled of course, and fiddled
with her hair. *O James*. Truth is
I loved you even as a child...

O slick-black-panted wanderer holding
your belly in, your phaser gun
on stun, and eyes like Conference pears! You're not my type
but I undress you, and we fuck
and I forgive your pancake make-up and mascara,
the darker shadows painted round your eyes.
The lava-lamp goes up and down. We're
a strange unison. Politically
Mismatched. Our mutual friend
The Doc takes notes. *Go easy Bones!*

Scotty is beaming and shouts *Energise*,
and all of a sudden you remind me
Of my dad, my brother and my mum,
my body rising like a shadow from the past
on top of you. As I press your arms behind your head
I drape my breasts so that you
brush my nipples gently with your lips almost
involuntarily as we boldly go. Come slowly, Captain,
and we do, with both our pairs of eyes tight closed.

SERVICE WASH

For six months now I've washed her clothes,
The old favourites, the new acquaintances:
One large bag of colours, one small bag of whites.
By now I've got to know the oyster camisole,
The chambray trouser suit, the pink silk blouse
That has its own expensive scent, the purple jogging suit
That smells of sweat and traffic. Her knickers
With the blood left on. Sometimes I think about her
And the way she does her hair, wanting to know
The thousand things about her that I don't already know.
The bell-boy says she's often out, that when he tips his hat
She smiles. My wife would kill me
If she knew the way I thought. *Pervert*,
She'd say. And then the rest. Perhaps she's right.
With the place to myself one afternoon
I tried a dress of hers, all fresh and newly ironed,
And then felt warm and close to her. I could have cried.
My breasts hung empty, huge pink satin flowers...

Mostly I keep myself to myself. Head down
And my back's covered. Christ knows, I need the job.
Sometimes, though, just sometimes, it can get too much
                                        and absent-
Mindedly I mismatch my clients' socks.
That gets them ringing for *Room service!*
Never her. I think she's like that, likes
To wear them odd. Once an old bloke
Sent me down a note which said that socks
Were Lost Platonic souls. I like the way that sounds.
Perhaps one day I'll say the same to her.
I'd love to make her laugh. Sometimes I see her smiling

Through the steam. Then she dissolves. Love's spectre.
There's no end to what you learn down here.

Sometimes I think an afternoon will last for ever.
Sometimes I think the world is flat. Go on. Convince me.
Sometimes I think I'll fall in love again.

The Best Individual Poems

Sally Baker

FAKE LEOPARDSKIN COAT

Where I come from the word is *Tart*
mouthed in the same breath as
What does she think she looks like?
but I love the feel of it, slipped
over shoulders over satin; long
for red lipstick and platignum, hoops
for my ears. I cannot resist.

In the café a woman is helped
to her chair and brought tea.
Windows steam. A mother and daughter
in matching track suits smoke
by the door, the same life lived over twice.
My coat sidles on the chair back, proud,
where I can touch it, spot side out.

At the bus stop a woman in green
has done up her hair in tights, her cheeks
rouged a fierce red. She sings.
I blow her a kiss, dreaming of sixty
and outfits to come. The courage of colour,
of shining out from the ordinary.
What does she think she looks like?

All day I have it near me, my coat,
laid in my lap in the car,
subdued and sleepy, stroking the fur
and folding my hands in the sleeve.
Something of me survived the journey
away and back, through years. The words
I am home on my lips, wherever that is.

Seamus Heaney

Cities of grass. Fort walls. The dumbstruck palace.
I'd come to with the night wind on my face.
Agog, alert again, but far, far less

Focused on victory than I should have been –
Still isolated in an old disdain
Of claques who always needed to be seen

And heard as the true Argives. Mouth athletes,
Quoting the oracle and quoting dates,
Petitioning, accusing, taking votes.

No element that should have carried weight
Out of the grievous distance would translate.
Our war stalled in the pre-articulate.

The little violets' heads bowed on their stems,
The pre-dawn gossamers, all dew and scrim
And star-lace, it was more through them

I felt the beating of the huge time-wound
We lived inside. My soul wept in my hand
When I would touch them, my whole being rained

Down on myself, I saw cities of grass,
Valleys of longing, tombs, a wind-swept brightness,
And far-off, in a hilly, ominous place,

Small crowds of people watching as a man
Jumped a fresh earth-wall and another ran
Amorously, it seemed, to strike him down.

Tobias Hill

The City of Clocks

Slaughter-month. The road is down
and the telephone clacks like knitting.
Departure is set back for days.
We play mah-jong to kill the time.
The pieces are made of bamboo
and seal-bone, green as oxygen,
and the back-cloth of evening

is stitched with violet bats. Breakfast
is kedgeree, served until noon.
In the hothouse, hydrangea
open like fists, their fingertips
litmus-paper touching the dark,
fleshy and bruised, testing soil
for acid and its violence.

We are returning to the city
where every room has an echo,
each echo, pitch. Whistle right,
and walls thrum like wine-glass,
crack. I pack boiled eggs,
a thermos, keys, plastic money.

All our maps are obsolete.
Along the oceanside, sinkholes
have cratered the new shopping malls
with sea-caves where waves slap like bombs
in the salt dark, and the arcades
reek of sewage and bladderwrack.

The metro surfaces for this,
follows the Bolivar Arcade
to a station lit with blue light,

Insectocutors in hot mesh.
They slap fat beetles in the dark,
spit sparks like old televisions.

This is our destination,
the city of clocks. Cover your ears
and you can hear the watches tick
in syncopation with your heart.
No two clocks are ever in time.
If we hold hands, our pulses chat

against one another, like teeth.
We sit and listen to the years.

Jenny Joseph

In Honour of Love

In your honour I have cleaned the windows
Of four-months' sorrow-flung obscuration and dirt
And cut my hair and thrown away old rags
That make cupboards foetid, suffused with miserly pain.
I shall wipe the mould out of the corners
Rub down, prepare to paint;   in your honour.

And in your honour
Am throwing out old nastiness with the floorboards,
Memories of hurt, *lèse majesté*
Along with the shards and glue, useless and hard now.

As if for new love turning a new leaf over
I will pick off infestation up to the minute.
At this time of budding give a chance to cleanliness
Make beds freshly in garden, and in the house
Fresh covers; as if with hope square corners
In expectation, in honour of your coming.

For your comfort and in your honour
I have laid by stores and funds of robustness
Sweeping despondence out with the spiders' coatings
Disinfecting anxiety, self-pity
The damp that clads, sours and eats the woodwork.

I think it isn't true that ghosts return
Only to ruins and to broken things.
Shy visitants that start to come with me
Along the track I make you from the past
By thinking of you, you would never bear
Burdens you could not shoulder when alive.
You'll still want cheering, self-reliance, comfort
The big wheel pulling up the hill, hearth cleared,

Coal ordered, landlord dealt with, 'sociables',
And so to welcome you and keep a place
For your reviving influence to bide in
I move within the chrysalis of doubt
Wound round for Winter comfort, for survival.

In honour of love, in hope of expectation
I leave behind drab covering that kept me
Safe through the Winter, safe and solitary.

The grub without its carapace is needed
Pale and soft and vulnerable, for birds
Shining and voracious.   So,
I am persuaded, every time a fool.
Well, something must feed the remorselessness of Spring.

The skin will burst, so you should see light wings
No dirty brown slough. The bad times swept away,
Place ready for the prodigal,
                              and be damned the peril
The piercing light and the brief high flight will bring.

Ashes, when you have gone, burnt bits on the lamp
That lit you on your way, but in your honour
As you pass by the window, love – bright flame.

Les Murray

The Shield-Scales of Heraldry

Surmounting my government's high evasions
stands a barbecue of crosses and birds
tended by a kangaroo and emu
but in our courts, above the judge,
a lion and a unicorn still keep
their smaller offspring, plus a harp,
in an open prison looped with mottoes.

Coats of arms, plaster Rorschach blots,
crowned stone moths, they encrust Europe.
As God was dismissed from churches
they fluttered in and cling to the walls,
abstract comic-pages held by scrolled beasts,
or wear on the flagstones underfoot.
They pertain to an earlier Antichrist,

the one before police. Mafiose citadels
made them, states of one attended family
islanded in furrows. The oldest
are the simplest. A cross, some coins,
a stripe, a roof tree, a spur rowel,
bowstaves, a hollow-gutted lion,
and all in lucid target colours.

The rhyming of name with name,
marriages quarter and cube them
till they are sacred campaign maps
or anatomy inside dissected mantling,
glyphs minutely clear through their one
rule, that colour must abut either
gold or silver, the non-weapon metals.

The New World doesn't blazon well –

the new world ran away from blazonry
or was sent away in chains by it –
but exceptions shine: the spread eagle
with the fireworks display on its belly
and in the thinks-balloon above its head.
And when as a half-autistic

kid in scrub paddocks vert and or
I grooved on the cloisons of pedigree
it was a vivid writing of system
that hypnotised me, beyond the obvious
euphemism of force. It was eight hundred
years of cubist art and Europe's dreamings:
the Cup, the Rose, the Ship, the Antlers.

High courage, bestial snobbery,
neither now merits ungrace from us.
They could no longer hang me,
throttling, for a rabbit sejant.
Like everyone, I would now be lord
or lady myself, and pardon me
or myself loose the coronet-necked hounds.

The Other Poems

Neil Astley

THE HOUND OF THE BASKERVILLES

Master says obey, but I'll stand up
on my hind legs, though I sway like a drunk.
If I can't slip this leash, I'll see his eyes
bulging like a dog's, my jaw clamped round
his jerking arm: the fingers I once licked

I'll bite off, crunching knucklebones to taste
forbidden flesh beneath his salty skin.
I want to know the Moor. What held me back,
call it habit or the easy life, was
nothing to wilderness. I could have played

his pet, become the old retainer sprawled
across the hearth. But fire's in my eyes,
by torchlight they're red as coals. My mouth
glows sulphur-yellow, tongue lolling ahead
divining water, testing air for food.

I'm hungry but have kicked away the bowl
branded with his name for me. I'm hungry
as hell, for his damnation, not bondage
from tins, not meat the price of his abuse;
hungry to hunt down what I need, snatch it

on the hoof, hungry as the loyal poor
asking for change. I want another life.
He makes his answer with a gun: five shots
ring out in the dark, one grazes my ear.
He can't shoot straight. He's shaking like a leaf.

Closer, Master. Let me lick you again.
When I was a pup, he came to me at night.
He put it on my tongue. My clumsy teeth

flecked blood in drools of dangling cuckoo-spit.
One bullet left. *You feeling lucky, Master?*

Annemarie Austin

GOAT SONG

Tipped toward the light
that strikes his belly flush
so that the navel offers itself
as the lifted communion cup:

the goat drawn to the flame
– a moth to the candle –
to be held in the play of pain
by his ribbon-tied heels.

This is tragedy in the purest terms:
the perpendicular dive down
from the branches spread like arms
to the blood-puddled ground,

and the god turned artisan
at work with the flensing knife,
unpicking pelt and skin
beneath the sacrificial tree.

Stretched by gravity and agony,
his torso itself is a torch
consuming its very substance
to light the darkening forest

for a last suspended moment
while still the navel brims
and tilts towards us whole –
omphalos, about to be broken.

Connie Bensley

Personal Column

Married man would like to meet
girl, affectionate, petite,
for afternoon diversion.

Vicar sighs. He'd like to meet
married man. It's wrong to cheat:
he hopes for a conversion.

Jane writes off from school to meet
married man. He sounds so sweet
she longs for the excursion.

Blackmailer would like to meet
married man, to make discreet
enquiries re perversion.

Now his wife would like to meet
man – her eyes are cold as sleet –
she writes: I am a blonde, petite,
and spoiling for diversion.

Charles Boyle

VELCRO

There's a tribe, I swear it,
in the Syrian desert
who bury their dead standing up.

Every five years, a great sandstorm
rages; diviners interpret
the chattering of skulls.

*

Their warrior queen
models Armani. Their children
are force-fed videos

of the long march
out of Crittenden
to Zit. Their god is named

after the terrifying noise
made by the opening
of a hundred tent-flaps at dawn.

*

The acrid leaves they chew
every waking hour
produce a mild

hallucinatory effect
of the kind experienced
by publishers' reps

while driving on the M6

north of Carlisle
in light drizzle.

*

Because their topography
lacks high places
they have yet to invent

the ladder. Because
of the premium they place
on originality in art

no two toothbrushes, funeral masks
or wheels
are exactly the same.

*

Sex: *see under* alabaster;
Earhart, Amelia; Friday.
See also tongs.

It's not that they don't
enjoy it, but are often inhibited
by their distracting need

to rationalise the gap
between the gritty norm
and their culture's pellucid ideal.

*

Travellers are welcome
during the feast of Gordon
but should take care to depart

before the unwonted outpouring
of intertribal affection
is bitterly regretted.

*

Lifetimes have been gladly spent
mastering just one
of their sacred texts

by scholars who still confuse
the place names and numbers
that may also serve

as exclamations of endearment
with those that signify
disgust.

*

Ever since the cataclysmic
civil war
between al-Origbi and Philip

twins have been both shunned
and revered –
for the drear month of penitence

that follows their birth,
for the good times enjoyed
by the priesthood.

*

By night, suddenly,
the Blowman will come.
Directly above the spot

where he will ejaculate
the glorious seed of the ancestors
into the sand,

a cloud in the shape
of *Phoenix dactylifera*
will mushroom in the sky.

     *

The cache
of lighter fuel, soda siphons
and stolen cheque books

found in a ditch
by H. du Plessix Gray
is not, as previously supposed,

a bluff, a feint
to put off tomb-robbers,
but the real thing.

Alison Brackenbury

Hay Fever
For Robyn

Eyes swell, as from a blow; you cry.
I have to fight
To keep your dirty fingers out of eyes
Which almost close
As you stumble past the plumed grass of the lane
The choking elderflower, the painful rose.

What is pollen, anyway? you sniff.
The dusty air
Veined with its passages of gold, as if
You were given presents everywhere.
Summer, for which you longed, to which you raced,
You cannot bear.

John Burnside

HOME MOVIE

They are one generation away
from Gaelic, or Latin,
walking the orchards in spray suits and surgical masks,
their science fiction bodies catch the light
or thicken and set in the shadows, like evening dew,
unable to return, unless I wake,

and I am the one who has come
from the distant city,
stumbling upon their magic, their rams's heads and candles,
the singing at nightfall, the dance on the moonlit green,
their stubborn games
of death and resurrection.

I should have left the village reels ago:
as soon as I met the children on the cliffs
I should have guessed – that laughter in the grass,
their knowing looks, the whispers in their sleeves.
I should have listened when the doctor spoke,
clumsy and fearful, barring the surgery door,
and when his body washed up on the rocks
covered with stings and bruises, I should have known.

Now I am packing my bags in an upstairs room
while, somewhere below, the solstice will soon begin.
I still intend to take the next train out
– as soon as the midwife comes, in her starched white dress
to give me her blessing: an apple; a copper nail;
a name from the churchyard;
the dead in their cradles of drowning.

Barry Butson

Just Another Hieronymus Bosch Evening in Woodstock

Such a lovely, such a lovely evening
as he sets out the sun pink against
the tops of apartment buildings.
As their cars pass him, the people's faces
seem embarrassed behind air-conditioned windows.
Some lawns are cut a uniform green
and he wants to doff his shoes and
rub bare toes on such perfect order
in this accountant's city. Clusters
of babygirl clouds coo in a babyblue sky.

Twilight time in this math-minded city, he comes
to a schoolyard with ball diamonds carved and
gravelled in three corners and a game's
participants dispersing, one truck spinning
its tires in static art as smoke of rubber
settles onto those in cars still remaining.
He sees this from across the playground, but
the truck with powerful engine and special
transmission comes wheeling around the corner
towards him and he sees its driver young
with a moustache and ballcap clearly, in mood
neither foul nor elated. Just burning rubber
in suburban boredom.

A dog the colour of dairy creamer
of ignoble breed but substantial size
runs into the schoolyard and twirls in
dumb distress as if to query his master
behind on bicycle
if this is a reasonable dumping ground
for his firm turds. As if answered, the dog
performs a circular shit as the young man

on bike looks on and the poet walks on
taking notes in his head, thinks of scenes
from the work of Hieronymus Bosch, knowing
if he walked forever, from town to town,
country to country, he would meet creatures
that expel from caves bones and gristle,
feathers and excrement with the consistency
of accountants.

But he heads home instead as another young man
passes him running. When he looks in the direction
from which he came sees yet another young man
bursting in underwear only out of a house
waving a hammer in one hand, his other red with blood.
This man runs directly to the closest parked car
and smashes each window with the hammer
while blood runs down his bare leg
from a hand whose index finger hangs
from a ligament. "Fucker cut my finger off,"
he curses. "I was sleeping on the couch and the prick
comes in and...". As he for some reason tells the poet,
the owner of the car and his girlfriend arrive.

The owner attacks the hammer-holding, finger-hanging
victim-avenger and as they grapple the woman turns the sky
bluer with obscenities and kicks at the two of them.
The lawn they roll on is not clipped neatly and green,
but weedy and brown as a board.

As the pedestrian poet leaves the scene he hears
sirens in the distance and sees parting with his head
the curtains in the house of sliced fingers
a dog looking out. Looks like it's snarling.

Julia Casterton

Vipers in Love

It is a steep climb to the anchorite cells
through mists of brimstone butterflies, smells
of sage and juniper. Wild boar feed
near the path, brown, bristly, their babies
big as cats, and a dead viper, her underside
bright silver, lies at my feet
like a chaste and plaited wedding necklace

for a meeting that waits in the air. I follow you,
afraid, more tired, into these words, that come
like scented meat, or the reek of the birthing room
where everything begins. You are always ahead,
a little further in the trees, testing me onwards,
knowing I will come to you, to the cells
where monks endured a biting cold, and under that

a mute invisible love streaming down the slopes
of their mountain. As mine streams now,
moving dangerously through the branches, the olive and brown
of a viper waiting to whip me in the face.
Because I have chosen this, that gives me pain
and brings me naked to you in this bitter,
ruined, parched, once-holy place.

Linda Chase

Young Men Dancing

Who were those young men dancing?
And why were they dancing with you?
And what was the meaning of all that business
around the area of the pelvis, both pelvises,
I mean, since I saw you with two of them.
Two men, that is, with one pelvis each.
Though there's your pelvis too, to reckon with.
It made quite a show of itself out there
on the dance floor. Not to be overlooked.
Nor slighted in any way, sticking like a magnet
to the erratic rhythms of those young men,
their jeans curving and cupping and making
promises in all directions of things to come.

Which way to go, you must have asked yourself
a dozen times at least, as the young man
with the smile turned this way, and the
young man with the dreamy eyes turned that,
and you were dazed, in circles, spinning
this way and that way, brushing up against them
in confusion, body parts in gentle friction
sliding back and forth, nearly seeming like
you hadn't meant to do it.
Did you mean to do it?

Could they feel your nipples harden?
Did they know what must have happened
as your thighs began to stick together, throbbing
to the music? Thank God there was the music
you could hide behind and make it look like dancing.
I'm wondering just how much attention
young men pay.

Kwame Dawes

Communion

On first Sunday, with the grey metal
table covered in flowing white, the
decanter catching the light, red with

Wincarnis, and those loaves of hardo,
Christ's body before the miracle,
from the country church come visitors,

three kings and two queens, the kings glowing
in their pink and blue gabardine suits,
the queens all in white, beating their tambourines,

their antiphonal shouts stirring the congregation,
though some will not move for fear
their hips will lose decorum.

On first Sunday, the cup of salvation
bearing His blood is passed
from lip to lip in heavy tumblers,

while the congregation sings,
'The blood that gives me strength...'
Clarice smiles her benign way

on the grateful who have seen
her clairvoyance, this fantastic magic
that has not come from the delicate

pastries of the loafer and chalice,
but from the yam mounds, the
Warieka marl pits, the lignum vitae's

subtle voice, the jasmine, the cedar,

the mahoe. Clarice speaks from
the covered table, her bible with

its supple broken neck, wind
fluttering the pages, the power of the word
now cutting through bone, marrow,

the word resurrecting Lazarus,
the stone moving. The sisters
shudder and shout, while the brothers

groan to the belly-roll they feel.
It is coming, this wind and fire.
But here in the interim, in this lull

between the spoken word and incarnation,
the explosion of new mornings, enters
Thalbot, drifting like wind-borne newspaper.

There is no alarm on his arrival,
but the presence jerks up the heads,
and Clarice turns to this walking prophecy.

A tambourine tinkles. A baby screams.
Clarice points her finger to the dizzy
crows who dive nose first

into the Liguanea Plains, navigating
with their frantic tails the sharp,
sudden descent. Thalbot falls.

Clarice prophesies into his panting body.
The sisters gather and clean Thalbot's
body of residual spirits, the froth

of spit from his mouth and the grime
on his face. They feed him bread

and wine while Clarice falls into

tongues and weeping. Clarice sees
again the rain of crows from the sky.
Someone testifies the same vision;

the congregation sighs.
Thalbot rises slowly. Miraculously
the songs flow familiar from his lips

and tears seep constant,
streaking his clean cheeks,
salting his broken mouth. Amen.

Rita Dove

Blue Days

Under pressure Mick tells me one
of the jokes truckers pass among themselves: *Why
do women have legs?* I can't imagine;
the day is too halcyon, beyond the patio too Arizonan
blue, sparrows drunk on figs and the season's first corn
stacked steaming on the wicker table . . . . *I
give up; why do they?* As if I weren't one
of "them." Nothing surpasses these
kernels, taut-to-bursting sweet,
tiny rows translucent as baby teeth.
*Remember, you asked for it:
to keep them from tracking slime over the floor.*

Demeter, here's another one for your basket
of mysteries.

Jennie Fontana

EYE OF THE HURRICANE

you came
like a dream

blue eye
of the hurricane

and sowed seeds
of infidelity

you stripped
to the waist
and cleared
our garden
with my husband

I watched you
stack fallen creepers
and dead leaves
and cover them
with earth – to rot

pick flown slates
and broken glass
and tuck them safely
from the children

you hitched a strong
rope and shackle
round the storm torn
cherry tree
and pulled
it down

my daughter my son
poked woodlice
out of the dusty core

we watched them

"You have beautiful
children. You have
love," he said.

you came
like an angel
out of the hurricane
and turned my eyes
to the salt
catching sun
on my windows

Cliff Forshaw

A God Perhaps
"Ein Gott vermags."
From Five Poems After the German of Rilke
Sonnets to Orpheus
I, 3

A god perhaps. But it's not that simple
for a man to follow himself through guitar strings.
His mind is split. Contradictory strivings
are his heart's paths. At his crossroads is no temple.

Song, you teach us, it's not about desire,
not about asking for what can never be asked.
Song is being. For a god that's an easy task.
But when are *we* live? When does he trip the wire

that turns the earth and stars towards our being?
It's not enough, young one, that you love, that voice
bursts through, blooms upon your lips. Try remembering

to forget. It means nothing, whatever you've sung
so far. Real singing - the truth - is another breath.
Breath of nothing. Gust of god. The wind's lungs.

David Gascoyne

A Sarum Sestina
To Satish Kumar

Schooldays were centred round the tallest spire
In England, whose chime-pealing ruled our lives,
Spent in the confines of a leafy Close:
Chimes that controlled the hours we spent in singing,
Entered the classrooms to restrict our lessons
And punctuated the half-times of games.

The gravel courtyard where we played rough games
During the early break or after singing
In the Cathedral circled by the Close
And dominated by its soaring spire
Saw many minor dramas of our lives.
Such playgrounds predetermine later lessons.

Daily dividing services, meals, lessons,
Musical time resounded through the Close,
Metered existence like the rules of games.
What single cord connects most schoolboys' lives?
Not many consist first of stints of singing.
Our choral rearing paralleled a spire.

Reaching fourteen within sight of that spire
Unconsciously defined our growing lives,
As music's discipline informed our lessons.
We grew aware of how all round the Close
Households were run on lines that like our singing
Were regulated as communal games.

We sensed the serious need for fun and games,
What funny folk can populate a Close.
We relished festive meals as we did singing.
Beauty of buildings balanced boring lessons.

We looked relieved at times up at the spire
Balanced serene above parochial lives.

Grubby and trivial though our schoolboy lives
Were as all are, we found in singing
That liberation and delight result from lessons.
Under the ageless aegis of the spire
Seasonal feasts were ever-renewed games.
Box-hedges, limes and lawns line Sarum Close.

Choristers in that Close lead lucky lives.
They are taught by a spire and learn through singing
That hard lessons can be enjoyed like games.

Ann Gray

TIME

The clock has metal flaps half way through
the numbers. They are yellow and go c-lick.
I see fifteen forty five and know I have
lost half past two. Somehow I have missed it.
I worked so hard and watched so carefully.

I wonder if the court room will be full,
whether he will stand, pompous, self assured
and say he speaks for me. Will they listen
and believe him? The children are too old now.
After all these years, I thought that I was safe.

The road is sandy and the tyres slip.
The blue station wagon has run out of petrol.
I try to run, but it is further than I thought.
The pavement is hard and it is very hot.
The roads are wide and totally deserted.

There are plane trees with dappled trunks,
their leaves are weeping. Every street looks the same.
I run faster. Bathed in sweat, I feel icy.
My breath hurts. When my mouth opens
no words come out. I cannot feel my tongue.

If I do arrive, I will look fearsome.
I will not be able to persuade them that I am fit
to be a mother. He will be standing there
cool and supercilious. When he sees me

he will raise one eyebrow. They will smile.

He sent a letter. it said half past two on Friday.
I am not now sure that it's not Sunday.
Time has meandered through my fingers.
I open them. I close them. They are empty.

Sophie Hannah

The Mystery of the Missing

Think carefully. You sat down on a bench
and turned the pages of a small green book.
You were about to meet your friends for lunch.

> I turned the pages but I didn't look.
> It felt as if the bench was in mid-air.
> Whatever held me wouldn't put me back.

What happened next? You must have gone somewhere.
The wind was blowing hair across your face.
Perhaps you went inside and lit a fire.

> But people looked for me and found no trace
> inside or out. I saw the things they feared
> in the green book before I lost my place.

Surely they weren't afraid you'd disappeared?
Did they suspect you might have come to harm?
You could have reassured them with a word.

> I wanted to, but every word that came
> threatened to burn my mouth. I also knew
> that soon it would be over, I'd be home.

The sky closed in. You say you shrank, then grew,
then everything came back to you with ease.
You sat quite still, deciding what to do.

> Huge purple bruises covered both my knees
> But no-one acted like I'd been away.
> None of my friends asked what the matter was –

> Everyone else had had a normal day.

David Hart

THE SILKIES

Someone last Autumn put the evil eye on Mrs Kendrick
for hanging bright crimson knickers on the line
in sight of where the boats come in,

and as the word got around the island
still the knickers flew there,
and they flew through last week's luminous storms
and through the lovely day we had on Sunday
when Jock proposed to me. Nobody of us

has spoken to Mrs Kendrick all these winter days. My dream
last night told me everyone has been cleared out
and that in the stolen land Mrs Kendrick alone remains,
she is hiding in a cave
below the water line
diving and gliding and eating blenny and shanny with the seals
and whispering to them at the hurt reach of her voice,
It's all you've got
wear the sea close, then she bleeds
all the way home; she is wearing a room
where the plaster flaps off the walls
revealing pictures of the hosts of hell,
dead pelicans queue on the roof,
cupboards sag full of uneaten meals,
windows have layers of faces fingered into their dew,
yet the wreath of roses on the door
drips loveliness. Boats fill the harbour,

it's the time of year, Mrs Kendrick makes red hot jam
for any captain away from home that wants it
on his night toast, I kiss Jock

on his rough lips in the shadows.

Phoebe Hesketh

BOY DROWNING

Drowning is pushing through
a barrier like birth
only the elements are exchanged:
air for water.
Then, water for air,
my lungs
folded flat as butterflies' wings
struggled to expand
in a round scream.

Now I make no sound –
or they don't hear
water damming my ear –
drums, nostrils, eyes –
I fight like a salmon on grass
choked with a bubble.
I cannot rise
a third time.

Selima Hill

My Life With Men

The first man I attracted
was my father,
who people said was young:
how young he is!
But actually he wasn't. He was old.
I told my little friends he was the lodger.
Next, the man who called me
Schlobovitz
and worshipped me unstintingly.
They all did.
And then the man I found upstairs in bed,
who said he was my
Unexpected Brother.
Why do people have to lie like that?

And later on I met his friend The Man.
And then another.
I was off my head.
I never loved them but I wanted to.
I wanted to so much I thought I did.
So much, in fact, I even married one,
and went to live in Manland, among Men;
where other women,
wrapped and stunned
like meat,
introduced me to the long machines
we mustn't leave
on pain of death
all day.

We mustn't walk,
or even go outside.
(If anyone's seen "loose" –

without a car –
they're rounded up
and given clocks and pills.)
We mustn't talk –
except, of course, effusively,
every time the phone rings.
Then we must.
(As long as what we say
is not the truth;
as long as who we're talking to's
a stranger.)

Our flowers
are dead.
Our animals
are headless.
Our children
are for smashing against walls.
And when the day
has done the best it can,
with well-scrubbed hands
we set our plastic clocks
and slip
like liners
into dreamless sleep,
remaining almost motionless till morning.

Michael Hofmann

EPITHANATON

Last words? Probably not, or none that I knew of,
by the sea with your grandsons in another country
when it happened. A completed manuscript on your desk,

and some months before, a choleric note dashed off to me
cutting me off, it would once have been said,
for nothing I could this time see that I'd done wrong,

part of your *Krankheitsbild*, I suppose, an apoplectic symptom,
so that I felt injured for once, and on the side of the angels.
A tantrum, I thought, tenderly, pityingly, *kleiner Papa*.

But nothing articulate, grandiose, bogus and spoken,
no Victor Hugo or Henry James, no *Je vois une lumière noire*
or *Ah, the distinguished thing*. When I was fifteen,

I told you about the Grateful Dead, and you liked that,
even tried it out in German, where it sounded, predictably,
a little swollen and implausible, *die dankbaren Toten*.

You looked, James might have put it, not ungrateful yourself.
Mildly bitter, thinner, quite wonderful actually
(I'm thinking of *deadish*, an old beer adjective),

Russian, bearded, still more sharpness about the nose
as the Russian (Tolstoy or Dostoevsky, ask Steiner) writes.
Dead, as you'd lived – more power to your elbow –

in a short-sleeved shirt. This one pink and still pretty good
(I'm afraid there were none of your clothes that I wanted any
more,
not since I got too big for your purple-lined boots in 1971).

You were well-nigh inaccessible behind a screen
of potted yews that I had to barge through to reach you.
Sprays of pluperfect flowers at your head,

the swanky brass tag at your feet, Dr. Gert Hofmann,
for your work on Henry James, a pleasingly unintimidating
effort that came to light in your papers later.

We all wanted to bring you things, give you things,
leave you things. A plastic ivory elephant from my sister,
who mussed up your hair each time they drove a part through it,

a few crumbs of lavender from me. All of it removed.
A custodian (morbid and fussy and phlegmatic,
like a character from one of your books)

took out the alarmingly long screws from the coffin,
as though someone could be expected to try very hard
to get out or – you would have said – in,

and first stood there holding the lid, then on my appeal,
took it off and himself with it. I hardly dared touch you,
your empty open hands on the awful mendacious coverlet,

the ochre bodystocking pancake colour of you,
and then fearfully the base of my thumb grazed your hand:
I would never be that cold as long as I lived.

After the funeral music – brass I asked for,
probably wrongly – we said our *Lebwohl* to you,
the inappropriate expression hurt as much as anything.

I speared my flowers at my feet, a no-throw,
the *blaue Blume* of the Romantics, delphiniums, blue for faith,
and turned on my heel like a cavalier swain,

prematurely, unconscionably, with you still there, then, while my back was turned, you disappeared into thin air, *dicke Luft*.

Mimi Khalvati

AU JARDIN DU LUXEMBOURG (DETAIL)
after Henri Cross

If summer had its ghosts, gifts of wind
wind blows to you and whisks away,
then these two small girls

in pale pink flared
like two sweetpeas
I would take for mine and twirl them
to the balustrade...

Look how, squatting, peering down
they think the ground a river,
a winding in the gravel

whose underwater mysteries
like gaps between our memories
appear and disappear...

Like gaps between our memories
that reappear through tow-ropes
seemingly in reach, then, far out

where leaves are light
and light is fish
persuade us with a colour,
dissuade us with a depth

twirl them back through leaflitter,
parkland, crossroads, up and over
chimneystacks, birchsmoke, lavender

till, like gaps between our memories,
seed and dust and all wind carries,

they are seen at such a distance

we think them elemental
light, fire, air!

David Kinloch

Paris-Forfar

From the window of the Hardie-Condie Cafe, I see the ghost of a
rich friend of my grandmother drive down Forfar's Main Street
in a Rolls-Royce I was sick in as a child. Behind me the water-
colours of stick girls walking through trees are misted blobs per-
colating in coffee steam. Mother comes in like Scott of the
Antarctic carrying tents of shopping. The garçon brings a cappu-
cino and croissants on which she wields her knife with the off-
frantic precision of violins in Hitchcock's shower scene. Soon I
will tell her. Show her dust in the sugar spoon. Her knife gouges
craters in the dough like an ice-axe and she tells the story of nine-
teen Siberian ponies she queued behind in the supermarket. Of
Captain Oates who boxed her fallen 'Ariel'. The chocolate from
the cappucino has gone all over her saucer. There is a scene and
silence. Now tell her. Tell her above the coffee table which
scrapes with the masked voice of a pier seeming to let in some
waters, returning others to the sea, diverting the pack-ice which
skirts around its legs. Tell her a fact about you she knows but
does not know and which you will tell her except that the surviv-
ing ponies are killed and the food depot named Desolation Camp
made from their carcasses keeps getting in the way. From this
table we will write postcards, make wireless contact with home
and I will tell her of King Edward VII Land, of how I have been
with Dr Wilson and then alone, so alone, in day-blizzards just
eleven miles short of the Pole and ask her to follow me. I am
afraid she has been there already. She smiles like the Great
Beardmore Glacier and goes out into the street with stick girls to
the thirty-four sledgedogs and the motor-sledges. You are too
late. Amundsen is in Forfar. She has an appointment. Behind me
I can sense the canvases, the dried grasses pressed into their grain
like eczema on an open palm. Later I will discover her diary and
what I told her.

August Kleinzahler

Bruce Richard's Trip Down

So I buy a pig in a poke and sign on.
One thing I did know, it was a Hans Christian 38,
cutter-rigged with a big, old-fashioned, full keel,
about four and a half tons of it, which meant
whatever came our way we wouldn't be sinking anyhow.

Stan, the skipper, didn't have a lot to say
but I got a good feel out of him.
The other hand, Lowell, was a librarian
and right off strikes me as a dilettante.
He's read books, OK, and talks good nautical
but has a fat ass, and that raises a few questions.

We head out of Bellingham around ten in fog.
It's Labor Day Monday and, Jesus, the strait's filled
with pleasure craft trying to make Deception Pass
at slack water, a real narrow little shot
between Whidbey and Fidalgo Islands.
You can see the charter boats poke through the fog

as we make our way slowly among them and west
to the ocean, hugging the coast, three or four miles
off the Olympic Peninsula. The fog lifts
and all of a sudden there are those peaks
shooting up like to make your head swim. At 3
a.m. we make Cape Flattery, the far edge

of the continent, and steer to the open sea.
Next day we're into blue water, 'blue water sailors'.
Lord-O-Dear, it's pretty: clear, no debris,
no logs or kelp, no birds; maybe an albatross
and a couple of gray whales up close, pretty pretty blue.

Out a hundred miles, free of the shipping lanes,
we point south and pick up a northerly
on our stern. What we wanted was for the wind
to be on our beam, giving us a bit of speed
and lift, instead of a wind like this,
bagging the sails and making for lots of roll,

which puts me off my chow and keeps me that way.
The wind picks up to 20 knots on the fifth day
and the boat really starts rockin' and rollin'
in this harmonic motion you fight with the wheel.

But we've begun making time and head into the night
with the headsails up. By now we are well along,
maybe on line with Port Orford and The Heads
down the Oregon coast and the wind picking up steady.

Me and Stan trade two-hour shifts with the wind
gusting to 25. We turn on the deck lights
and drop the big headsail. All we have left
is the storm jib off the starboard with the wind
still dead north and increasing as we point due south.
Lowell's down below, which is right where we want him.

In the cockpit it feels like you're going 60
what with the wind and white water racing past
your ears when it's only 4, 4½ knots you're traveling.
Your senses play tricks on you about now,
fixed on the red dial of the compass, fighting off sleep,
only 10° to play with either side of downwind.

When you look forward you see the headsail silhouetted
against the sky, floating, like a wing in a dream.
Meanwhile, you're busy trying to pop the wheel
against each roll, and you don't want to lose the course
on a turn to port or the boat'll head to weather,
and if you're flat unlucky maybe broach.

When it finally turned light, not much after six,
you could see the waves, huge, forty-footers,
an unbelievable sight, white everywhere,
big graybeards with the wind blowing their tops
into spray. I make up my mind to heave to:
so I throw the wheel all the way over and lock it,
figuring the boat would hold a pretty good course

with the jib back-winded, riding over the tops of waves.
We were headed west now in a full gale
with the wind steady between 35 and 40,
or gusting to 45. I went below to rest,

but at 2 a.m. the boat got caught on the face
of a haystack, an enormous wave, forty foot
from crest to trough, and took a terrible shot
flat on its side, *BAM*. Whoa boy, that puckered my sphincter
and drove the cold wind of wrath down my corridor;
but all that keel weight went right under
and forced the rig back up: winch handles, half
the storm dodger lost; books, tools, kerosene...

Next day, the seventh, with the staysail back up,
the skipper decides to abandon the trough
and head south with the wind. By that night
the waves are quieter and farther apart
and we're able to turn around onto a reach
and limp our way in the direction of shore.

We raised a ship the next morning, a freighter
headed east from the Orient. They told us
we were a hundred miles farther south than we thought,
and seventy miles farther west. Stan had had us
dead-reckoned about level with Cape Mendocino.

That's where our luck began. We came round on a beam reach
that brought us all the way to San Francisco.

We wound up sailing past the Farallons just around sunset
and through the Golden Gate into Richmond Bay.
Man, that's a magical feeling, sailing under that bridge
with those big standing waves either side of you,
same as you find sometimes in white-water rapids.

The wind held strong all the way in to Sausalito
where we got the sails down, fired the engine
for anchoring, had us each a couple of beers,
and that's when I phoned you, cousin.

James Lasdun

EDEN

Winter, nighttime, Jane Street and West Fourth,
Three blocks east of the Hudson, brownstones
   trussed
In garters of lacy black wrought iron,
Steam-spooks and gravelled moonlight, frost...

It might have been the second night of creation;
Stellar silence, a triple-locked
Empty universe waiting for the first spoor
To lug its baggage five flights to the door –

For two days I didn't unpack.
I liked the ringing air distilled
Out of bare walls and empty shelves,
The whiff of promise not yet unfulfilled,

I could be anyone; I bought three vast
Elaborate tropical stems – a token
Of the man I was to become:
Freed, flamboyant, bigger-hearted...

I watched a tongue unfurl, fanned ganglia,
Dewlaps, a clutch of hatching parakeets
The room swarmed in a puce light –
I couldn't wait for them to die;

It seemed they never would: the coil and bloom
Convulsive, intimate; a masque of carnage –
Adam, Eve and Lilith, one stem each,
As if they'd sprouted from my own flesh.

In June the prehistoric gingkos
Swam veinless leaves through the greased, sizzling air,

We lay in the emerald swamplight
Listening to the monkey yelp of sirens –

Dawn was the dawn of time: Triceratops
Hauled its meat off the screen at Naturemax
And rumbled down Columbus.
I woke to hear it snuffling in the garbage.

Tim Liardet

THE HOUSE OF CORRECTION

Free me from my body's sloughing
With its tireless tide-measure,
From the rest and the whip of pleasure.
               Bernard Spencer

1.
Your softly striving pistons will shortly blow blue.
Poor girl. Because the speedometer doesn't work
You have to guess what speed you are rising to.
You're down on your springs. Such luggage makes you sway
From lane to lane with a soft occasional lurch
Which induces that crazy reproval of horns
On the expressway between him and me. Enough to say
The journey always funnels to a path of thorns
At either end, so overgrown. For so it goes.
Those nasty Shakespearian tines will snag up your nice clothes.

2.
I bought you a silver brooch of two kissing birds;
A gold cherub, a frog glittering in marcasite.
But they simply ended up with the cockateel's turds
In the bin amongst the fluff and onion skins
When we were discovered. Beneath the bin-man's feet
One was crushed, another was pinned on his overalls,
A stone in his sole as he hoisted the bins;
This is where love goes when the Council calls,
Manhandled out with the leavings to where
The kiwifruit and It grow a puff-ball of purple hair.

3.
Now you have come around that long sweeping bend
Between order and love, you've come south to south.
Your husband's golf-ball steeples in the wind.

At that very moment—the peak of the ball—
Your soft mouth is whispering into my mouth:
Let me go, let me go, wrap your feet round my feet.
Ahead lies more discovery—discovering all—
Deceit, discovery, deceit, the last of deceit.
The stranded man strains up at the wayward ball.
But in its widening gyre it cannot hear the golfer's call.

4.
So just lie in the conjugal sack if you must.
You made it. So lie where you lie, your back to his.
The bed-springs beneath you should be locked in rust.
You're awake, again. Over your shoulder his face
Changes into mine, to his, to mine, the hairline is
Receding and re-seeding like an even tide
Of longing and remorse, at an even pace…
Though every instinct is to move, I abide,
Attuned to the radio play of your ordeals.
I hunker in the shadow of your giant misshapen heels.

5.
Once, there was simply order. Each year upon
Yet another mirageous foreign beach you posed
Lankily in shorts, arms trailed, or shielding sun,
Your long legs ending where you worked your feet deeper
Into depths of warm sand, soothing your toes…
At noon, it is too hot to walk on. You work
Instead the deep runnels of your biro deeper
Into depths of pure cold white, a watermark;
Those ghosted shapes, scary and overblown,
Any earnest chic psychologist would certainly disown.

6.
Your grandmother's buried sackcloth is your judge.
Her brow—those puffing cheeks, those liver-spots—
Turn slowly away, the priesthood's. Your cheeks smudge
Blue into her apron, all her strength forsakes

You; her family's offspring gurgle in their cots,
Weightless, helpless, in the shade of the priest.
The only daughter childless, still the old roots make
Your people your people. Avoid your mother's least
Oblique glance, the ills that enclose her.
The last few yards between us are your *Via Dolorosa*.

7.
By the way of hesitation you reached the gauze
Of infinite scope three times, unable to speak.
That weight upon your fingers, it is not yours;
Mouth airbrushed away, you cherish heavy rings,
And the flames of a thousand crackling wicks upon your cheek
Tear in the very slightest draught. Detached
From their collapsing fluid grottos, like wings,
They scatter one way. Through tears, you have watched
The wax dissolve its walls and roll to meet
The hard perfection of a Saint's remote cold marble feet.

8.
As a child you had often dressed in your sleep:
That crooked tie, that collar—the sleepwalker's work.
Now you dream the whole family forbids you to leap
Naked on to the stage, to dance. The stalls revolt:
You shiver in the wings, while your sisters cavort—
Dressing, undressing in sleep, amount to the same.
Naked with me all morning—veiled in guilt—
You rush to get back to work by the way you came
But your shirt is crumpled, buttoned up wrong.
You've played the half-dressed sleep-nude now for much
                                        too long.

9.
When I drive it is you who dips the beam,
It is you who slips us up gently into fifth.
In the dashboard lights we're sadder than we seem.
We prolong the latest goodbye, since goodbye

Means pausing, at every lay-by for another kiss,
Each one the last. I come back on the train
To find the duvet as we left it, piled up high—
All night, your ghost hanging over me, the rain
In its soft perpetual and dying fall
Holds the hovering strange light of your smile on the dark wall.

10.

Love released you for a frenetic while,
Stood you in high heels, kept you rising. You
Shed a stone on its diet, happy, juvenile.
But all the while the monsters nudged at your roots,
Guilt, remorse. They coaxed you very slowly, drew
You down into their world—clouded, subfusc—
More and more of its water weighing your boots
When you tried to rise clear, but failed. The cost
Was to go deeper, every time you went higher
Towards the very giddy scorched superlatives of desire.

11.

Gethsemane—above the dark and swirling Tay—
Is reached, you say. Away, you pause on the bridge:
The black floods pour invisibly, stray
Under the great arches with a large roaring voice.
Any way you look at it you're out on an edge—
On both banks the thorns more widely divide
To leave you the bridge, yourself. Is there any grace
Down there in the waters that mutter and chide?
You are caught—erased, though heaven-sent—
Beneath the monstrous figures of a stucco firmament.

12.

In both our gardens at once the laburnum's gold flows;
Nine hundred and ninety days of your backstreet calls
Can't bring you close enough. For so it goes.
I call you back at the call-box. The racket of
Your city almost drowns your voice in roaring squalls—

Then it takes you away. Of the one much-abused
Your accusers whisper: *still cuckolded, lacking love.*
The tickets for the concert never get used.
Our blue water suffers your oil-slick of sin.
But any amount of showering will not wash me off your skin.

13.
Come home. *Come home.* The injunction swings both ways.
Both ways at once you drive the contraflow.
The troubled Catholic daughter stays, but strays;
The voice of reason, growing hoarse, under duress,
Drowns in a crowded hall of catcalls. You go
To Mass, pray for three, for something cleaner;
Those eerie engrams none of us will possess—
The water rises daily, in a closed container.
You confide in the cockateel, which never sings.
Over your strong beating heart the heavy thurible swings.

14.
As if to make the almost cautious almost rash
Your blinds do not quite meet, nor reach the sill;
To morning scaffolders (who croon and crash)
They yield a glimpse of one unlevel bed that leans
Too far over to one side, and always will.
The blinds do not quite meet, though barricades,
And all the evidential bedding, sheets and stains,
Is left to the baroque disfiguring chambermaids,
Desire, Deceit and Guilt, come for the wash,
Speaking through their low tar catkins of impending ash.

Michael Longley

THE SCISSORS CEREMONY

What they are doing makes their garden feel like a
    big room.
I spy on them through the hedge, through a hundred
    keyholes.
He sits in a deckchair. She leans over him from behind
As though he were a little boy, and clips his fingernails
Into the newspaper he balances between his knees. Her
White hair tickles his white hair. Her breath at his ear
Might be correcting his sums, disclosing the facts of life,
Recalling the other warm cheeks that have hesitated there.
He is not demented or lazy or incapacitated. No,
It is just that she enjoys clipping his fingernails
And scattering them like seeds out of a rattly packet.
Are they growing younger as I walk the length of the
    hedge?
Look! The scissors ceremony is a way of making love!

Glyn Maxwell

YOUNGER THAN THAT NOW
(for the Folk at the Barn)

Open the door one crack and you are backstage.
The closest of the bright unanswering faces
You love and know, but away down the crowded passage
They get much gloomier, longer to recognise.
      Your shyly whispered guesses

Widen and die like cigarette fumes in a hall
Of cleanly livers. You did not know you were holding
Your breath when it broke clear, and there is no wall
To touch, there are only inhabited crackling clothes
      And soon the dizzying feeling

That you must walk through here through the way of them all:
The girls of the frozen chorus, the mouthing page,
The hero bare, the jacketed devil, the cool
Chanel of the goddess, the flirt of the woods, pass on
      Away from the terrible stage

That grinds its young in the light or blows them dark
Like birthday candles, move down corridors
Where the murdered glance from a brilliant mirror and back,
By vast and icy rooms with bills of plays
      That call you to old wars,

Past centuries of dresses coldly hung
In line, rich girls speechless at the affront,
And cards of luck and photographs of song
Pinned to a blistered board, pass by the wires
      That lead from what you want

Away to the grids and terminals of power,
Pass by yourself in brown and broken glass,

By planks and crates at the foot of a storage tower,
By what seems rubbish to you but will be of use,
    And then the rubbish. Pass

Right to the end of the theatre, some last
Green paint-spattered chair by a bolted door.
Far from the lives of the young indignant cast
Or wrenching earshot of beloved lines,
    Sit yourself down there.

Feel like a boy the burden tremble and slip.
Empty your pockets of work and empty your ears
And nose and eyes of fashion. Summon up
Whatever remains. If nothing remains amen,
    But blink no appealing tears,

For here you sit in the foreground of the world.
And what you sing in the dark is the plain song
Of men alone: unobservant, innocent, old,
And blue with wonder, and beating a way back home,
    And over before long.

Bernard O'Donoghue

GOING UP ON DECK
for Steven Rose

Either because there's a finite number
Of viruses, most of which you've had
Already, or because your immune
System loses the stomach for the fight,
As you get older, you don't catch colds so much.

Nor do I any longer care about
That corner of the road, avoided
For twenty years because of the back
Of a navy coat. *We* could have foretold
That the heart grows old: we sped it on its way.

But isn't every kiss a Judas kiss,
Pointing the way ahead? You can't survive
For ever on the life-enhancing pain
Of the happy time recalled in misery;
Fireside warmth becomes as tantalizing

To the speckled shin. Twenty years
Is a good innings for nostalgia,
Before dedication wilts. Nowadays
I find myself inclined to linger
In the cabin's mild protection,

While affection cools for that fool
Who stood by the rail, inventing
A waving, waiting girl in a long scarf,
And seeking inspiration in the slung
Sack's smack against the solid sea,

Or verbalizing the waves' sweep by the side,
Imperious as the driving gannet. He's

There still, I'm sure, held in place by the dark
And the sudden wind at the corners,
And the chain's rattle in the lifeboat's throat.

Katherine Pierpoint

Going Swimmingly

The blue-rinsed pool is full of rhythmic, lone strokers.
It drew us in from the edges as though it were blotter-dry and we
    were rushing liquid.
Swimming, an occasional, unseen toe contact
Seems to come long after the other solemn face bobbed by;
The body lengthens, a pale streamer drifting out under a
    Chinese lantern.

Standing in the pool, blinking and pinching your nose, brings
A strange slewed perspective down to the wavering floor –
Firm, cream shoulders, telescoped to no trunk,
Standing on skewing, marbled shimmypuppet legs,
Fatdappled with fallen blue petals of curling light.

Swimming, everything is simplified.
The eye level so low, a baby's out along the drunken carpet.
A rhythmic peace, of rocking and being rocked,
Plaiting yourself into the water,
Ploughing an intricate, soft turtle-track along the undersurface,
Each stroke a silver link in the chain that melts behind you.

Sheer weight and size of water!
Remembering some geography and its clean, cross-section
    diagrams –
The sea is an upside-down mountain of water,
An upturned yogi
Alive with pulling, fluid muscles;
A pressing city of water; a universe;
The town pool is an inverted block of flats, something
Gathered and gently milling. Container for a small revolution.

Hands trying to pray. Legs slowly trying to fly.
Simple, straining juxtapositions –

Waterbuffalo! Hovercraft! Starfish!
The water on fire in volcanoes and set in earth in amber!

The swimmer broaches a strange but yielding density;
Leans quietly into a huge, enfolding flank.
Reaches over, forward and out; to re-test the limits,
Smooth the limbs,
Of a rediscovered lover.

Milner Place

I said to him you know the rain
has hardly stopped the last three days

He said in Patagonia there are shrews
that excrete perfume so divine that bees
are drawn from natural flowers to the shrew's
sable tongue for it to steal the golden harvest

I said maybe it will clear up this afternoon

He said in Kuala Lumpur some nights the frogs
achieve such pitches that their songs burst amber
jars of rice wine and fruit flies get drunk
frogs feed insatiably the lizards too

I said the greenhouse effect will melt the ice

He said that in North-East Australia crocodiles
have a special penchant for the blues and if
you play Miles Davis to the setting sun they turn
white bellies to the rising stars and greet
the tropic night with little grunts and purr

I said that in Estonia there are wolves
that gather every Candlemas to hold
a howl-in and their music causes bears
insomnia but passing caribou react
differently and dream erotica

He said I think you're right about the rain

Peter Porter

CONNECT ONLY

I'm drinking illicitly
from a bathroom mug
in a Writers' Retreat
some Montepulciano d'Abruzzo,
not my favourite wine
but usually the one
inside those carrier-bags
sold on Italian stations
to hungry travellers,
and I am back again
with a pretty companion
I don't get on with sharing
lunch en route to Ferrara
where we won't sleep together
and I'm happy to allow
this memory of the train
to remind me of the time
my wife and I encountered
a man who entered our carriage
at Padua and masturbated
against her thigh all the way
to Venice, and I wouldn't
say anything to stop him
out of embarrassment
and he justified me
by pointing beyond the causeway
and welcoming us—'Eccola
Venezia'. A simpleton,
he more or less resembled
a beautiful Renaissance male
in a portrait on a postcard,
and my wife is dead and she
didn't resent what he did,

only my cowardice, and I
need forgiveness of them both
which is why that postcard
is ample occasion and reason
for my mind to wander to
other postcards and other
parts of Italy and on to days
before we went from England
for our holidays and the kids
were tucked up for the night
and we'd sneak out to find
a pub and look to see if each
could somehow find the key
to the other's doubtful heart
and failed, I'm sure, but still
felt closer for the try,
yet somehow this won't fix
and back comes drink, the days
of scouting bottles locked
in drawers of knickers or
stuffed behind old shoes,
the death watch born of life—
all this was years ago
but who believes in time
whose body bears him on
to where all memories meet
or has the style to face
the picture of himself
when wine must have a stop?
Now gadarene the words
run headlong down the page,
old symbols no one trusts—
alas, we're trained to tell
back to ourselves at night
the endless consequence
of being alive and hands
revelling in such trust

reach out as well they might
for wine in bottles rich
with the red threads of death.

Peter Redgrove

The Moths

Palpitations – the moth-beats
Of the heart in the clambering weather
Wrestling with itself.

The moth lies down on the windowpane full of light
In its bath of lights.

I look out of the window past the moth
Like some gigantic inhabitant rising from its unconscious mind.

What does the unconscious mind of a moth resemble?
The conscious mind of a devoted naturalist.

That is why the moths come to him like inhabitants
Of his unconscious when he lays his white sheet down in
                                       midnight
Over the grass and shines his car's headlights on it;
They speed to their baths of light.

And here come more moths over the estuary,
They stagger over the roof of the house of light built without
                                         hands,
And they settle in its garden of white lawn.

Before he thought of blacking his face they came to him,
To its whiteness, and sipped from the fountains in the pores.

Now they come to his body-heat
When he lies down in his bedsheet.

They will eat him like candy even to the bones,
He will fly away on their wings;

None of the wicked will understand,
But the wise shall understand.

Robert Rehder

ON THE NATURE OF PHYSICAL LAW

When I take the new shampoo
From its box, I hesitate

To throw the box away.
This is the strong force

That holds the nucleus together.
I save old tickets of all kinds

To mark my place in books
And very often I stop

Half-way through.
Separation is a problem.

I do not like to walk
The same way twice

And am uncomfortable parting from
Old copies of *Le Monde*.

They are stacked around the house
As if history was

A black and white lichen
Or topological problem

Of folded sheets in n dimensions,
Finely printed cascades,

Giant banknotes
Of an obsolete currency,

Last year's snow,
Secrets hidden among ferns.

The urgent bulletins
From the Hochschule St Gallen

That announce
A new course in investment strategy

Or seminar about Mexican debt
On wonderful green

And deep purple paper
I pass to Katherine,

Hoping that she will keep them –
Use them in a collage

Or anything
To save them from extinction.

My old teabag is deposited
On the edge

Of the draining board
In a gesture of not quite farewell –

Pygmy rhinoceros,
Pony express mail-bag,

Sketch for a monument.
There is something behind everything.

Somewhere Stendhal says
That he wasted thirty years

Waiting for inspiration.
Write every day. Hold on.

Maurice Riordan

LAST CALL

Home late, his house asleep, a man goes to the phone,
and from habit, expecting nothing, touches the Recall.
But this time he tenses to hear the electronic scramble,
the pause before the lottery digits fall into place.
At the other end, sure enough, he hears a male voice,
no one he recognizes, repeating *Hello, hello?*
He can hear background piano, Chopin or John Field,
establishing a room, smoke-filled, larger than his,
where wine in a discarded glass is losing its chill,
while the voice continues, good-humoured, persuasive:
Come on, say something. He tries to picture a face, a hand,
to fit the voice, still in his ear, still going on, *Last chance...*
He hangs up, his own hand shaking with intimacy.

Ann Sansom

Mine Host

I had a name but they have swallowed it,
downed it by the pint. And I have swallowed
so much that I might give way. I might.

Tonight, I just contain myself. I go on
pulling ale and nodding Aye and Gerraway?
with one ear cocked against the margin
of a conversation, on the edge
of mild debate and brewing trouble.

I have the punchlines, the final say,
Time, gents. Sup up. It's Time.
And they subside, obedient, cowed:

I shepherd the unsteady, hold the door.
And someone might catch hell outside,
someone at home might come it, question
what's been spent, someone might wonder
what I buy one half so precious as I sell...

I slam the bolts behind. I touch hands,
gently, with myself and rock and sing
I wish I loved the human race, I wish...

I tilt my head, Yes, my good man? Yes, Sir
Yes? Yes? Sometimes it will not pass.
The juke box dies. A glass of rum and black
burns sanctuary and in my mirrors
in my bottles me and me

and my cathedral settles.
Then I bucket the fag ends and ashes,
wipe the bar and spread the towels;

I gather up the dregs and slops
and tip them in my special cup.

May Sarton

Crawl under the roots of a tree
No one needs you any longer.
You the destined solitary,
You can sleep away the hunger
That is tearing you apart,
Woman with an open heart.

No one's mother, no one's child
Living in unsheltered space
Be the stranger reconciled
To the absence of a face,
To the end of family,
Never able to say 'we'.

Woman with an open heart,
Close the valve now, dull the beat
Sleep away the stop and start.
You will find enough to eat,
Friendly trees to shelter you
And the ocean often blue.

You will comfort with a word
Others who are lost like you,
You will celebrate a bird,
Sing the song of falling snow
Become balm for every hurt,
Woman with an open heart.

Carole Satyamurti

STRIKING DISTANCE

Was there one moment when the woman
who's always lived next door turned stranger ·
to you? In a time of fearful weather
did the way she laughed, or shook out her mats
make you suddenly feel as though
she'd been nursing a dark side to her difference
and bring that word, in a bitter rush
to the back of the throat—*Croat / Muslim /*
Serb—the name, barbed, ripping
its neat solution through common ground?

Or has she acquired an alien patina
day by uneasy day, unnoticed
as fall-out from a remote explosion?
So you don't know quite when you came to think
the way she sits, or ties her scarf,
is just like a Muslim / Serb / Croat;
and she uses their word for water-melon
as usual, but now it's an irritant
you mimic to ugliness in your head,
surprising yourself in a savage pleasure.

Do you sometimes think, she could be you,
the woman who's trying to be invisible?
Do you have to betray those old complicities
—money worries, sick children, men?
Would an open door be too much pain
if the larger bravery is beyond you
(you can't afford the kind of recklessness
that would take, any more than she could);
while your husband is saying you don't understand
those people / Serbs / Muslims / Croats?

One morning, will you ignore her greeting
and think you see a strange twist to her smile
—for how could she not, then, be strange to herself
(this woman who lives nine inches away)
in the inner place where she'd felt she belonged,
which, now, she'll return to obsessively
as a tongue tries to limit a secret sore?
And as they drive her away, will her face
be unfamiliar, her voice, bearable:
a woman crying, from a long way off?

Robert Saxton

The Farmyard Crocodile

Settled in one of the crypts or vestries
    Carpentered like a bureau's secret drawers
In the ziggurat of hay in the great dutch barn
    Shortly I'll lay my head. If you come by
With your torch and see my shoes in the corridor,
    Look in on me: see that I've come to no harm.
From my attic of hay I've been watching you
    In the failing light, alone down there
In the farmyard, too distressed at having lost
    The fluorescent green crocodile they bought you
At the fair to notice the change coming over
    The animals. While you've been staring down
Into the black water of the cattle trough,
    Into which you could no sooner plunge your arm
Than you could plunge it into solid rock,
    Their storybook slave-clothes have been melting,
And their eyes, large and small, have started
    Their bore-holes into our comfortable night.
After you've gone to bed, shall I clamber down
    The giant steps of the ziggurat and creep
To the cattle trough, very quietly so as not
    To spring open their eyes? In the morning
You'd be amazed to find your toy on the stone rim.
    In the cave of your hand (I'm dreaming now)
It might even glow again, but altered forever,
    Like an animal's eyes after its first beating,
In which our offences smoulder like the wasted years.

Adam Schwartzman

LIBERAL

Wanting to forgive among the flower-beds
the liberals hoped for justice but loved their children more

and had decent anguish in their oaklands
whose fair thoughts were not extraordinary.

They saw their sons grow strong, their daughters beautiful,
ate on the patio, notched heights on their door frames.

They knew to hate the tracks in unprotected fields,
dust stirred up in other people's gravel streets,

so fought part-time to give it all away
and be free to walk in smaller gardens guiltlessly.

Penelope Shuttle

OUTGROWN

It is both sad and a relief to fold so carefully
her outgrown clothes and line up the little worn shoes
of childhood, so prudent, scuffed and particular.
It is both happy and horrible to send them galloping
back tappity-tap along the misty chill path into the past.

It is both a freedom and a prison, to be outgrown
by her as she towers over me as thin as a sequin
in her doc martens and her pretty skirt,
because just as I work out how to be a mother
she stops being a child.

Charles Simic

History Lesson

The roaches look like
Comic rustics
In serious dramas.

Matt Simpson

Prufrock Scoused

Less juss shin off me an yooze
seein as ow its as soddin borin as
someone avin der appendicks out.
Lets juss bugger off down ere
where thee ardlee is no one
where the moanin minnies toss n turn
in the doss ouses or Yatsiz Wine Loge
where thee spew der rings up
an piss on the floor down streets
that go fuckin on-n-on like some beady-eyed
bastid big-ears luckin fer a barney
an tryin t catch yer out not knowin sumpin.
But dont gerrin a tizzy doin yer ed in
juss fuck off down there anyroad.

Ders diss posh do wid lah-di-dah judies
janglin about ow thee once-t knew John Lenin.

Foggy out. Luck arrit tru d winder
like sum jigger rabbit, sum jowler prowlers
smudgin the glass or lappin up yuck
outer d gutter scratchin the bin bags
slinkin off den jumpin up orl ov a suddin
curlin roun the ouses before gerrin its ed down.

Yeah OK it can do dat
when it wants to if it likes an no messin.
Yooze yerself cud purron yer come-in-the-jigger suit
an go out an marmalise someone or not. Depends.
Tons of bleedin time – hours – fer the both ov uz
t juss dick around or not, even...
dreamin yer life away or buckin yer ideas up
before tuckin in t yer bacon butties.

Orl dem Lady Mucks is still at it!
Wen ar thee gunna give over eh?

Arent I right tho? Yiv gorr-ages
t cack yerself if thats what yer fancy
y cud even scarper if y wants.
Ah God eh, the bastids-ll call uz Baldy Ed
(bald as a bleedin melling thee-ll say!)
Me wid me duck suit on, tie an everythink,
orl decked up like the Cunt of Monty Cristo
(bet thee call me friggin Neck Ends!)
Just oo the fuck am I den?
I'm no redskin with arl the answers thats f sure.
I cud juss snuck out off ome
an wotch Blind Date on the telly.

An yer not gettin one over on me neether!
I been there ar kid!
Orl them brew ups I put down me
an everyone clammin up wen I walks in.
So juss tell uz oo the fuck am I, Wack?

Its the way thee orl gorp at yiz
as if yiv juss come over, callin yer
a wally behind yer backs.
OK, so I'm a dosey-arsed bastid
so wot? Its ardlee werth
undoin yer flies for, never mind
takin off yer kecks.

Dem posh judies, I know der likes
fur coat an no nickers the one arf ov dim.
(Cant elp fancy the one or two tho!)
Ten t one dat ones Oh-dee-Klone over der
is puttin me off me sarnies.
Mind you some bobby-dazzlers too!
But oo am I tell me?

Any case worra y gunna come out wiv?

Sumpin like diss? Excuse me luv
burr'I seen orl the owld geezers on ther tod
smokin ther Woodies. Reckin dats enuff do yer?

Shud juss pack it orl in! Dats about
the size ov it. Eer yare tart, wanna fotie?
The avvo, the evenin avin a birrova kip
jerked off if ther jammy or praps
shagged out, or simplee angin the latch, eer
nex terruz on the arth rug.
After arl the swiggin an the bevvyin
I don't think I'd get me end away now anyroad
eevin if I wantid. Like someones sliced yer ed off
an brung it in on a tea tray like yer John the Papist.
Makes no odds, no skin off my nose.
I'm norreevin in the make-specks wen it cums
t judies. Anycase the chucker-out looks
like eez gunna yocker on uz on the way out.
Gods onest trute, I woz creemin meself.

Ooze t say itd do any good after anyow
scoffin yer cornflakes, sippin Typhoo
orl dem orniments on the winder ledge
the pair ov uz yakkety yackin over ow good
a shag it woz or not, then gabbin away
like Father Bunloaf about capital ell friggin Life
as if Lazzerus cum back from the Udder Side
t say worrits like. So bleedin wot? Speshly if
some ot kecks tart turns roun an sez
call tharra dick!

Big ook eh? Know worr-I mean like?
After orl the arsin about...ard to purrit
inter werds... but like seein yerself
on ome videos pullin soft arsed faces.

Wot wud be the use if sum
snotty nosed little Tilly Mint went an told yer
y werent on afterorl?

That thingee by Shakespeer, Amlit is it?
Well dats not me, I'm no Rhubarb Vaselino
I'm more y can-lad, doin odd jobs
sweepin up an tha, sumtimes even
suckin up t the blockerman, now an aggen
a titchy bit lah dee dah, burr OK reelly
sumtimes wen I'm not coddin meself
a birrova twat.

Not gettin no yunger neether. Worrabowt me
all toney, kecks up t the knees at New Brighton?

Do I go the Swenys fer a short back-n-sides?
Gerra curry from the takeaway? Juss you see me
in me dago kecks cockin an ear t the seagulls janglin

thee bloody ignor me them lot!

I seen them messin about roun Gladstn Dock
an dive bombin the Royl Iris.

Reckin I need me bumps feelin
gettin orl gooey over the thort of a feel up
in the sand dunes at Formby.

'Eh yooze mate d wanna nuther bevvy?'

Harry Smart

Our Pretty Garden

When all around was green and pleasant summer garden-land,
all roses, all sweet and gentle lawns, our garden was a wasteland,
green, but savage-set with thistles, nettles, lupins and
the Giant Hogweed's brutal weal.

We scythed it and we strimmed, we dug it and we burned the
waste
in heaps. Our fires were petrolled into twilight,
smoked evil yellow palls across the street.
We made, one afternoon, such kapnorrhagic pyroflux

of broom and bramble, nettles hacked and raked into a
sulphurous mass,
our neighbours intervened. We quarrelled,
words misshaped as mutant snakes of smoke
across the wall between us, venomous, then later made our
peace.

The battle turned when we discovered paraquat
which, sprayed, made even our vile grassy weeds give up
their greenery. Their finery was browned in August and
September
saw them start to rot. We waited for fine days

that would give us chance to burn the slaughtered plot;
they never came. In late November first snow fell upon the town,
the hills had been white-capped a fortnight by that time. Finally
we used a flame-gun but the ground – dead grass – it hardly
burned,

just crackled as the tops were scorched.
Where the gun had passed the ground would smoke,
pale vapour from the blackened lawn. Soon, in sole charge

of the flame-gun and having been instructed in its use,

the art and craft of lighting it, its own adjustments, times and
moods,
I wandered lonely as a gunner round my felted lawns and
borders,
ripping streams of flame through stem and stump
and tussocked weed, through green leaf and through whitened
stalk.

Where the opened ground had borne a crop of seedlings
sprouting into autumn air I painted flame upon the neophytes.
So was it grand and great to grill my land,
such furious tillage gave my spirits great increase.

I torched a bank of dead grey grass,
I moved upon a border of new growth.
I turned aside a wooden board
and saw a dozen fat and glossy snails

where the flame had played. I flamed them once again,
their shells spit-spat the tortoiseshell veneer away
and stared as pure white eyes in dead reproach.
Still I flamed them till they cracked like chestnuts in the heat.

I found a robin's corpse and I cremated it.
I watched the feathers melt, the legs reduce to two neat pins
of piercing whiteness in the crucible.
The eyes themselves were gone before I noticed them.

Poor robin, finding his refuge from winter's cold
within the flame-gun's blowtorch range.
The calcine robin settles into ash and earth,
a wreath of cooling embers where he lay.

Sam Smith

Important Information For Canoeists

Water exists in two planes,
the horizontal and the approximately vertical.
Umbrellas are inneffective
and interfere with the wielding of paddles.
Alligators will not be found,
although both can swim, in the same
climatic zones as elks.
Panic is started by a sudden
loss of balance. Remain seated.
Light is a commodity
and an instrument of ageing.
Jellyfish have no function
in freshwater. Neither goose nor grebe eat them.
Solitude expands the consciousness.
Loneliness makes transparent the skin.
Here you can be your identical twin.
Beaver have flat tails
and are incapable of rational conversation.
Canoes can be treacherous.
Place no reliance on shined talismans,
make sure your lifejacket is securely strapped
and trust in your own judgement.
Not to be recommended,
while afloat, under starlight or dense cloud,
is the cooking of macaroni.
Also the fermentation of blueberries
and distillation thereof, even if apricot-flavoured,
is strictly speaking illegal.
For warmth a fire of fircones
can be built at the water's edge.
(Take care not to let the parent tree
witness the incineration of its progeny.)

Coition, of whatever variety,
is best conjoined on ungiving ground.
When following waterpaths of moorhen
and coot, be wary of contamination by crayfish.
Be patient; and ignore
the panic-stricken flight of waterfowl.
You are the cause.

Charles Tomlinson

WEATHER REPORT
for Brian Cox

First snow comes in on lorries from the north,
    Whitens their loads—an earnest of that threat
Cromarty, Mull, Fair Isle and Fasnet
    Have weathered already. It has passed
Down the Pennine chain and choked Shap Fell;
    The Snake is lost and every moor
In Derbyshire under a deep, advancing pile.
    It covers the county, dwindling south,
But the wind that carries it, overshoots
    The frontier snow has mapped. It is the wind
Seems to be blowing the sunlight out
    As it roams the length of the whole land,
Freezing the fingers of tillers and of trees,
    Until it curls back the tides off Cornwall
Telling the snowless shires they too must freeze,
    In this turbulence that began as Swedish air
And has turned in the translated atmosphere
      To the weather of the one nation we suddenly are.

Greg Woods

A Blind Man Looks at a Boy

The smell of oranges – I could have been satisfied with that.
The spray – like an impolite but fragrant sneeze. I could
Have introverted all my senses, had I any sense.
And felt a thumbnail underneath the peel prepare to flay
The pulp. No need for an ending, no need to taste the fruit.

I could have sat here at my desk and been tempted by
All manner of profanities, my fingers dancing on
The blotting paper, sticky but as chaste as apathy,
The orange rolling on the carpet out of reach.
It would have been a simple life, a hive of discipline.

Instead the tilt of my tentative radar locates
A baffle at the centre of the room. My voice
Comes back to me a little late, diverted, each syllable
Coerced into the service of a boy's physique.
'Who's there?' reverberates on drumskin, naked abdomen.

A slight acoustic flurry, amplified within the vortex
Of his navel, makes me sound concussive, tremulous.
I seem to have decided – and been right – he won't reply.
The light is thick, life short, the stillness of the evening air
Transfigured by the delicate pomander of his balls.

Gerard Woodward

The Starter

I was stranded at the beginning
Of everything, up a ladder that had
Been kicked away, but still there,
A bank manager refusing the overdraft,
A station master failing to delay
The train, I brandished my flag
Like one but I was already history
To them, the first page
Of their history, or one drowning
Or waving, or surrendering,

Or Lord Raglan at the lip
Of the valley realizing his error
But denying it. I was seeing
The end of winter, bad weather
Departing, a storm of horses
Taking the first fence, leaping
My own heart and raising turves
On the far side like hats
Thrown at some fiesta.
They'd ruined the spring.

All those small wagers worthless
Like the bulbs that were fooled
Into coming up early only to be
Bitten back by normal frost.
I blamed the grey, buckacting
At the tape, and then I nearly
Throttled a celebrity, but I suffered
On my own private Tyburn from where
I could see the horses, tiny
Now, as if I was six o'clock
And watching the second-hand,

Waiting for its return,
Waiting for the return
Of disappointed thunder.

Aintree's infinity of mud.
It's been heavy going. I watched
The winner who wasn't burn in his steam.
If I wasn't the beginning then this
Was the end. I wake at night,
My quilt a mass of printed hooves,
And sweat in the monstrous silence
That is the absence of horses.

That it should end like this
After such a good start, my life.
Who knows where a circle begins
And ends? At least I can see
The winning-post. The furlongs flash by.